Goodbye Phone, Hello World

Goodbye Phone, Hello World

Goodbye Phone, Hello World

60 Ways to Disconnect from Tech and Reconnect to Joy

by Paul Greenberg

Illustrations by Emiliano Ponzi

CHRONICLE BOOKS

SAN FRANCISCO

Library of Congress Cataloging-in-Publication Data available.

ISBN 978-1-4521-8452-4

Manufactured in China.

Design by **Lizzie Vaughan**.
Typeset in Brandon Text and Sentinel.

10 9 8 7 6 5 4 3 2 1

Chronicle Books publishes distinctive books and gifts. From
award-winning children's titles, bestselling cookbooks, and eclectic
pop culture to acclaimed works of art and design, stationery, and
journals, we craft publishing that's instantly recognizable for its
spirit and creativity. Enjoy our publishing and become part of our
community at www.chroniclebooks.com.

Chronicle Books LLC
680 Second Street
San Francisco, CA 94107
www.chroniclebooks.com

"Life is available only in the present moment."

—THICH NHAT HANH

CONTENTS

Beginning

My son was born in 2006.

The iPhone was born in 2007.

They have been competing
for my attention ever since.

I always knew it was wrong to
steal a moment to look at my
phone instead of my son.

But I thought I had plenty of moments...

REALITY CHECK

Secure attachment begins in infancy, when children take visual cues from their parents' gaze. In a 2017 study of children aged seven to twenty-four months, it was found that infants and toddlers had higher levels of distress and were less likely to investigate their surroundings when their parents were on their mobile devices.[1]

And then my son was twelve.

My time as the father of a small
child had come to an end.

What had I given my device
that I could have given my son?

Like the average American,
just under 4 hours a day.[2]

Every day.

Two months out of every year.

Two years out of the dozen
my son had been alive.

Gone.

And now my son was twelve.

He told me it was time he got his own phone.

Most of his friends already had one.

Eighty-nine percent of the 40 million
American adolescents already do.[4]

Was there anything I could say?

Is every child now required to forfeit
those same hours, months, and years?

More, actually.

Teens now spend on average more than
7 hours out of every day on their devices.[5]

Nearly the sum of their entire
time outside of school.

I researched, I reflected, I despaired . . .

I learned that my phone is not there for
my amusement or my son's education.

It's there for our marketable distraction.

Its purpose and our purposes are at odds.

I learned that the bank account of my time,
which my device had drained over the last
decade, was the currency of something
that had recently come to be called
The Attention Economy.

A system of commerce that draws its
profits by laying claim to our focus and
selling it on the open market.

Of course, people have always been
trying to use our time for their profit.

The first newspapers that sold advertising
took a few minutes a day away from the
people of the 1800s.

Radio in the 1920s and '30s
took a few more.

Television in the '50s, '60s, '70s,
and '80s took still more.

Our minds and media have always
been a little like host and virus.

The host tries to resist invasion.

The virus adapts to penetrate the
host's defenses.

The host adapts again and resists
the new infection.

The virus adapts again and penetrates . . .

There's something new now.

The virus wants to take over the host entirely.

Today a smartphone brings the moment-
merchants past all our defenses into
every second of our waking lives.

Every tick of the clock can be sold.

Every minute can be bundled
and shopped to a third party.

And the power of the moment-
merchants has grown apace.

The CEOs of the largest Attention
Economy companies have amassed
fortunes comparable to those of
the pharaohs of Egypt.[6]

Pyramids of unfathomable wealth built
out of the bricks of our consciousness.

The next time my son asked me
about getting his own phone,
I tried to tell him all this.

I wanted him to see his thoughts
as precious, private.

I wanted him to keep his time for himself.

"If the phone is so bad," he asked, "why are
you always on it?"

I wanted to tell him that it wasn't my fault.

I wanted to tell him what Cal Newport had said in *Digital Minimalism*, that "people don't succumb to screens because they're lazy, but instead because billions of dollars have been invested to make this outcome inevitable."

I wanted to tell him that when you look into your phone, you think it's just your two eyes looking at a screen.

What's really happening is that 10,000 programmers' eyes are looking back at you, following you, tailoring your environment so that you'll keep looking.

But nothing I *said* meant anything to my son.

I had to *do* something.

"What if I quit?" I asked him.

"You'll never quit."

"I think I'll quit."

"No you won't."

"If I quit, will you stop asking to start?"

He didn't answer.

So I quit.

At the phone store, the saleswoman
keyed in the codes to switch me
to a flip phone.

A "dumb phone," some people call it.

"Did anyone ever ask you to do this? Go
backward instead of forward?" I asked.

"Nope."

"Do you think it's a good idea?"

"I mean, maybe. But how are you gonna get
places?"

I thought of all the places I once got to . . .

One July day, long before the smartphone,
I asked my friend Molly to meet me

at 11:00 a.m.

on the ninth of September

in the Piazza Margana in Rome.

She was there.

And I thought of all the wanderings of my
friends and lovers during my teens and
twenties. All the places they'd disappeared to
and all the magical ways I'd found them again.
When Laura D., with the long blond hair and
the operatic voice, who never capitalized her
i's, was heading to Florence, I wrote a letter
addressed to her at the central post office
like this:

LAURA D.
FERMOPOSTO
FLORENCE, ITALY

And she wrote back!

Dearest Paul,

i was feeling so,
so lonely, and then i went by
the post office
and i found your
lovely letter. i was
so thrilled...

Before smartphones,

when you thought of the people you loved,

you thought of their faces.

And you thought of their handwriting.

My son and I left the store
with my new dumb phone.

A minute later, I reached in
my pocket to check something.

There was nothing to check.

There was only my son.

"Now what are you going to do?" he asked.

"I have to think about it."

And I thought about it.

What could I do with 4 extra
hours every day?

Two extra months every year.

How could I change my life?

How could I transform my world?

How could I show my son a better
way without that greedy shard of
metal and glass in my pocket?

I can report back, many months later,
that I was able to answer these questions.

The conclusions I reached were
sometimes very new and
sometimes incredibly old.

As in thousands of years old.

Many of them had been
reached by others.

There was no shortage of books
about the problem.

But here's the thing.

The most helpful pieces of wisdom
I found were buried in books so long
that the phone-distracted individual
would never get through them.

So, here is a book for those who can't
quite find their way back to books.

A handful of crumbs (with pictures!)
to lead you home to yourself, your own
mind, and the life you can experience
only in the present moment.

*"It is better to do one's own duty
without distinction than it
is to do the duty of another well."*

—KRISHNA TO ARJUNA,
THE BHAGAVAD GITA

I.
Finding Purpose

It's said that smartphones make the tasks in our lives easier, faster, more efficient.

But what use is a life lived efficiently if it has no core, no organizing principle?

It is the essential rock of human purpose that smartphones so dangerously erode. By diverting our natural curiosity to more and more random and less and less meaningful tasks, they diminish our energy and time, leaving us lost.

By following the trails of marketing and manipulation, we are doing the bidding of others rather than that of our souls.

And while it might just seem like a moment here and a moment there, those lost moments add up.

Over 10 years, the average smartphone user will burn through about 14,000 hours of screen time. This is more than the 10,000 hours Malcolm Gladwell wrote in his book *Outliers* are necessary to master a skill. Gladwell notes, for example, that at least 10,000 hours of practice are required to become an "elite pianist." Some have taken issue with Gladwell's tidy formula. Not everyone has the native talent to become an elite pianist.

But who knows what talent lies within you? Will that talent come out by staring at a phone? My guess would be no. "The point is," Gladwell later wrote, "natural ability requires a huge investment of time in order to be made manifest."[7]

Search Out Your Practice

In the ancient Sanskrit sacred text *The Bhagavad Gita*, the god Krishna, incarnated as a charioteer, instructs the young warrior Arjuna on how to live a fulfilling life. He tells Arjuna that the divided mind is an unhappy mind but that "[w]hen a person is devoted to something with complete faith, I unify his faith in that form." Mastery through practice is faith.

By replacing some of your device-divided time with unified time, you begin to lay down your own path.

→   PRACTICE

Take a month to experiment with different practices that could be sustained over time. Is it the piano you once played? The watercolors you've always wanted to paint? Try taking 15 minutes of what was your smartphone time and dedicating it to that practice. Evaluate your feelings after each short session. At the end of a month, choose the practice you want to follow and pursue it consistently throughout the next month, increasing the time you spend on that practice by 1-minute increments each day as time allows. You can always change to a different practice, but try to sense if your shift is due to a deeper avoidance.

REALITY CHECK

Interruption from devices is now a regular feature of the modern working day. According to a 2008 UC Irvine study, workers who function in a frequently interrupted state experience more stress, higher frustration, and more time pressure, and must expend more effort than workers functioning in an uninterrupted state.[8]

Focus on the Elements of Good Practice

You may not become an elite pianist if you give up your phone, but consider the essential elements of practice outlined in "Expert Performance: Its Structure and Acquisition," an essay by K. Anders Ericsson and Neil Charness.[9]

Individuals who succeed in mastering a skill generally:

Practice with the specific intention of improving, not just repeating.

Practice in a sustained manner over a period of years—in most cases, as many as 10 years.

Introduce into their practice a means of being evaluated.

Question Distraction and Where It Leads

A likely reason you are turning to your device is avoidance. Avoidance of pain, of something vexing, of something embarrassing. But as the psychologist and meditation instructor Stephen Cope writes in *The Great Work of Your Life*, following distraction to its end seldom ends well. Summarizing Krishna's advice in *The Bhagavad Gita*, Cope writes, "The impulse to eschew the unpleasant leads to avoidance; avoidance leads to aversion; aversion leads to fear; fear leads to hatred; hatred leads to aggression. Unwittingly, the oh-so-natural instinct to avoid the unpleasant becomes the root of hatred."[10]

→   QUESTION DISTRACTION PRACTICE

Next time you pick up your phone, take a moment to think about the thought you had just *before* you did so. Focus on that thought, that person, that task and hold it in your mind. Look into it rather than avoid it.

"Can you keep the deep water
still and clear so it reflects
without blurring?"

—LAO TZU, *TAO TE CHING*

II.
Strengthening the Mind

That the smartphone first appeared in the United States was both surprising and inevitable. America is a country built on the concept of Manifest Destiny—a nation organized around constant expansion into new territory.

It's an idea that has unfortunately bled into other countries, other ideologies, allowing humans to push the natural world into a smaller and smaller corner of the planet.

And now that humans have exploited the majority of the planet's physical territory, that same tendency has turned toward the unclaimed territory of the mind.

But this mind is your land.

You must occupy it fully to own its power.

Sleep

If focusing on a practice proves difficult, it might be because key foundations of your psychological health are being undermined by device use. The blue light emitted by smartphones suppresses the secretion of melatonin—the hormone that helps us get restful sleep.[11] Harvard researchers and their colleagues conducted an experiment comparing the effects of 6.5 hours of exposure to blue light compared to other light colors. The blue light suppressed melatonin for about twice as long as other colors and shifted circadian rhythms by as much as 3 hours. This translates into more than 900 hours of lost sleep per year.

→ SLEEP PRACTICE

Avoid looking at screens beginning 2 hours before bed. Consider adding a blue light shield to your device to reduce exposure during other times.

Dream

If we sleep better, we'll dream better. Carl Jung believed that individuals who engage with their dreams come to realize that dreams collectively "form a coherent series in the course of which meaning gradually unfolds of its own accord. It is as if not one text but many lay before us, throwing light from all sides . . . which gives us all the clues we need to correct any possible errors."[12]

This was part of what Jung called "the night-sea journey," the pathway to the inner workings of the most hidden parts of an individual's soul.

REALITY CHECK

"A dream not understood
is like a letter unopened."
—The Talmud

Instead of looking at your phone first thing in the morning, establish a dream journal. Put a notebook, a flashlight or camper's headlamp, and a pen next to your bed. Document your dream as soon as you wake and stay in the dark if possible. Try to render your "night-sea journey" as truthfully as you can, with special attention paid to things that at first seem insignificant. The Jungian analyst Colette Aboulker-Muscat recommended dividing the pages of a dream journal in two, with words on one side and images on the other. This first step can set you on a course for creative thought throughout the day.

Daydream

Dreams can open the mind to more explorations of self during the day. In other words, daydreaming.

Quiet, undistracted time might at first seem like nothing. But, as Cal Newport points out in *Digital Minimalism*, quiet nothingness is essential for a part of the brain called *The Default Network*.[13]

This is the part of the brain that allows us to self-reflect and go deep into our minds. It's also the part of the brain that gets inadvertently turned on and wearied when we use our devices. While you're engaging with a screen, your mind often spins and grinds its gears with no result.

→   DAYDREAM PRACTICE

When impatience arises with an empty moment, the author and meditation instructor Sylvia Boorstein recommends saying this simple mantra:

May I meet this moment fully.
May I meet it as a friend.

Do Nothing for Creativity

Nothing is something. In fact, out of nothingness flows all somethings. It's in reaction to nothing that we find our motivation to reach within our consciousness and make something substantial out of the void.

In his fictionalized incarnation, Jerry Seinfeld famously pitched a television show about "nothing," which of course was a circular reference back to the show *Seinfeld* itself.

But *Seinfeld*, the show, wasn't about nothing.

It was rather about what we make of nothing.

Which, for the real Seinfeld, turned out to be quite something.

Nearly everything.

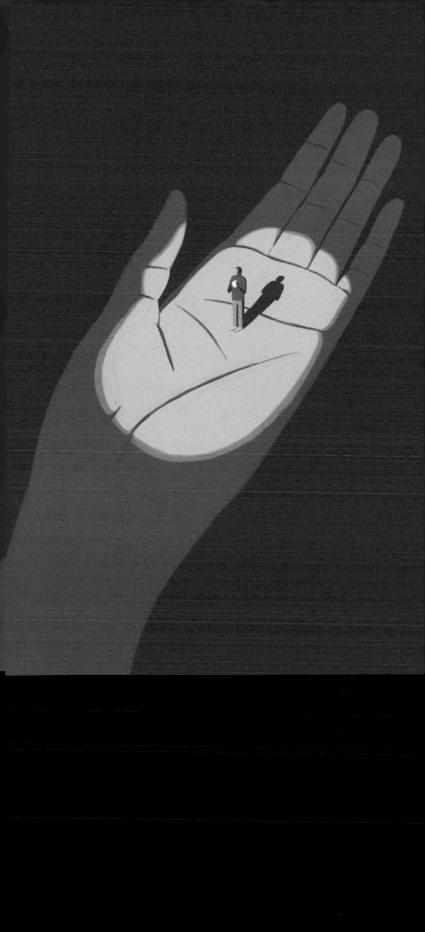

In 1967 the psychologist J. P. Guilford pioneered something he called the "Alternative Uses Task," more commonly called the "Paper Clip Test."[14]

In the test, subjects are given a common household object (like a paper clip), 2 minutes, a pen, and a piece of paper and told to come up with as many alternative uses for that household object as possible. The test not only measures each test-taker's creative range but also serves to expand the subject's way of thinking. Next time you find yourself in a Seinfeld-esque situation with nothing on your hands, make something of nothing and try the Alternative Uses Task with an object in your field of vision.

Do Nothing for Love

From nothing also flows an awareness of our true feelings.

Shakespeare's King Lear asked his three daughters,

"Which of you shall we say doth love us most?"

Cordelia, the one daughter who truly loved Lear for Lear and not for his kingdom, asked of herself:

"What shall Cordelia do?

Love, and be silent."

When Lear pressed her for an answer, she replied,

"Nothing, my lord."

"Nothing will come of nothing, speak again," insisted her foolish father.[15]

But for Cordelia, everything came from nothing.

Lear's question forced her to go deep into her mind to discover that she loved her father limitlessly, inexpressibly. Comparable to nothing in this world.

Restart a Deep Reading Habit

The average reader, reading at a speed of two hundred words per minute, would take approximately 105 hours to read Marcel Proust's *In Search of Lost Time*, Volumes 1 to 7.[16] With a year's worth of device time repurposed, a reader would get through Proust's chef d'oeuvre more than 14 times. With over $1,000 saved from not using a device, the ambitious reader could travel annually to Illiers-Combray, the setting of Proust's first madeleine-soaked memories.

Proust aside, "deep reading," that is, reading long-form paper-based books, turns out to be deeply beneficial. A 2016 study published in *Social Science and Medicine* found that book readers lived an average of 23 months longer than nonreaders.[17] "People who report as little as a half-hour a day of book reading had a significant survival advantage over those who did not read," said the senior author, Becca R. Levy, a professor of epidemiology at Yale. "And the survival advantage remained after adjusting for wealth, education, cognitive ability, and many other variables."

Leave the house with a hard copy of reading material. It can be a magazine, a book, or a letter from a friend. Include reading material as part of your daily checklist of things to bring when you depart home. Be compassionate toward yourself if you experience fatigue after just a few minutes. If your ability to read long-format print has atrophied, it can take a little time to build the muscles back up. And pay it forward, too. As Jenny Baum at the New York Public Library put it, "Just handing a book to someone is powerful. It's so simple that I sometimes forget."

Reconsider Paper

A 2018 meta-analysis of multiple studies that included over 100,000 participants found that reading comprehension increased dramatically when readers switched from online to paper-based reading.[18]

Why is this the case? The internet reader is forced to make myriad tiny decisions with every link she encounters. "Do I click and do something else or do I keep reading?" she must constantly ask herself. A nagging and wearying thing. "These decisions," writes Catherine Price in *How to Break Up with Your Phone*, "are so frequent and tiny that we really don't even notice they're happening.[19] But we can't make split-second decisions and think deeply at the same time—the two thoughts use different and competing brain regions."

Timothy Shanahan, a leading scholar on reading, occasionally tries this thought experiment: He takes the same text and reads it online and on paper and evaluates his feelings about each experience. Try this on your own—feeling is believing. In Shanahan's own experience, reading online feels "more like skimming." Shanahan further recommends "setting up reading environments that are maximally pleasant for you ... there's the expression being 'lost in a book.' That's what we're going for."

ReRead

The novelist Vladimir Nabokov said that "a good reader, a major reader, an active and creative reader is a rereader."[20] Reading something a second time gets you past the author's artifice and into his or her essence; the calling that inspired the writing in the first place. And rereading can also be used to recall a time before smartphones when you read for pleasure in a less distracted state. The ideal book to read again now is something you read before the smartphone existed. As you reread, try to retrace your emotional steps as a reader. Tether yourself to that earlier, more focused self.

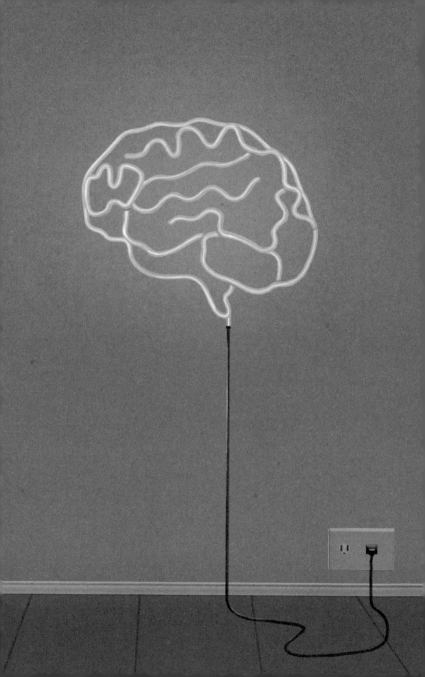

Memorize

It's well established that a strong working memory improves the mind's ability to acquire more memories. In addition, a working memory actually aids in creativity. Perhaps this is why the Greek goddess of memory, Mnemosyne, is said to have given birth to the nine muses. Memory is the mother of creation.

This is backed up by hard science. In a test of individuals tasked with creative assignments, Dutch researchers found subjects performed worse on their assignments when their memories were in poorer condition.[21]

→   MEMORY PRACTICE

Take small steps toward rebuilding your active memory. Memorize directions to a destination or your closest friends' phone numbers. Expand to embrace your chosen daily practice. Memorize a minuet, a sonnet, or verb forms of a language. Five minutes a day will do. Your mind will be stronger because of it.

Meditate
(without a watch or phone)

As 2,500 years of Buddhist tradition proves to us, meditation does not require an app. In fact, when we use meditation apps we can unwittingly find ourselves drawn back into the phone's myriad distractions when the timer rings. An important part of meditation is bringing the mind-state it fosters into the non-meditative parts of our day. By definition, using an app walls off "meditation time" from "regular time," when really what we want is for the two to blend together.

→   MEDITATION PRACTICE

The good thing about a meditation practice is that it can be begun anywhere at any time for any length of time. You needn't sit in a lotus or any other uncomfortable position. A chair is just fine. And instead of using your phone for a timer, try using a stick of incense, which burns for about

30 minutes—about the length of time neurologists believe triggers a shift in brain activity and a turn toward calm.[22] Can't stand 30 minutes? Cut the stick in half. As your meditation session ends, give your attention to the ember at the end of your incense stick. Notice how, in the last moment of its existence, the ember flares brighter. Keep this image with you throughout the day to bring you back to the presence you had during your meditation.

REALITY CHECK

"When we pause, allow a gap and breathe deeply, we can experience instant refreshment. Suddenly, we slow down, look out, and there's the world."
—Pema Chödrön in
Taking the Leap

Marvel at the Power of the Mind

Tech boosters sometimes note that today's smartphone has more programming power than the space shuttle.

But the phone is far from all powerful, especially in comparison with the human brain.

In terms of sheer computational resources, we can compare synapses in the human brain to transistors in a phone's computer chip.

By this metric, the brain wins handily—not only are brain synapses much more complex and powerful than transistors, we have 100 trillion of them, while a phone only has a billion transistors.

Phones may seem fast, but they're only fast at very specific things and are no match for the power and breadth of the mind.[23]

III.
Strengthening the Body

Many people use smartphones to track fitness and strength training.

But as Manhattan-based personal trainer Doug Joachim puts it, "Tracking apps are useful for quantifying one's baseline. Initially they act as motivators but the effect often fades over time."

Personal trainers also note a kind of reverse placebo effect or what they call a *nocebo*.

"Some individuals reward themselves with extra food when their app tells them they met a goal," Joachim continued. "Many times this reward negates their effort."

To counteract the "nocebo" effect, use your exercise regimen as a way of connecting with your surroundings and friends. Developing exercise habits that build bridges to the real world has the benefit of bringing about stronger mental acuity even as you improve your physical well-being.

In the end these are much more significant goals to realize than merely hitting the goal set for you by an app.

Turn Your Phone-Based Obsessive Exercise Regimen into a Gentle, Meditative Practice

Regular exercise indisputably improves your health. According to the Mayo Clinic, regularly running or walking for 30 minutes can reduce your blood pressure by 4 to 9 points. The importance of this can't be understated.[24] The Global Burden of Disease Study, the most comprehensive international analysis of epidemiological data ever completed, concluded that the #1 risk factor for death in the world is high blood pressure.[25] And of course there are many other reasons to exercise regularly that range from improved mental health to better sleep to reduced risk of cancer and diabetes.

But exercising with a phone can work at cross purposes to the health benefits of exercise. Checking email repeatedly has been found to raise blood pressure in subjects an average of 5 to 10 points.[26] And increasingly, research is revealing that goal-setting fitness apps tend to lead us toward obsessive-compulsive "streaks" that are often out of sync with the needs and capabilities of our bodies. We push ourselves to meet trumped-up goals, injure ourselves, and short-circuit our fitness plan before it can be put into full effect.

→   EXERCISE WITHOUT PHONE PRACTICE

Instead of looking at your exercise routine as a phone-regulated striving toward a goal, view it instead as part of your meditation practice. Most meditation retreats include periods of walking meditation as a way of bringing mindfulness off the cushion and out into the world. To experience exercise as a kind of walking meditation, take note of your breath as you would in sitting meditation. If your mind wanders from the breath, remind yourself, gently and without judgment, to return to the breath.

REALITY CHECK

"I have two doctors, my left leg and my right."
—G. M. Trevelyan

Circumnavigate

Certainly we could all use more offline exercise time. What could you do with 1,400 extra hours a year, fitness-wise?

In 2017, the globe-circling Scottish cyclist Mark Beaumont smashed the world circumnavigation record by riding around the planet's land mass in 79 days pedaling 16 hours per day for a total of 1,264 hours, just under a year's worth of smartphone usage.[27] The average human couldn't match Beaumont's feat, but with some training, maybe a device-free rider could make it halfway.

Seeing half the world traveling at low speeds with head up is a whole world in and of itself.

Work Out with a Friend Instead of an App

Working out with a friend instead of an app is certainly more rewarding emotionally. But trainers and athletes also find considerable performance benefits. As Arnold Schwarzenegger put it in his autobiography, "a good training partner pushes you to handle more poundage and gives you incentive to grind out more reps per set. . . . Workouts are more fun with a partner as well as more competitive . . . you challenge each other."[28]

Brush for an Extra Minute

At the very least, claim 1 extra minute from your phone and brush your teeth for an additional 60 seconds.

You will reduce your risk of contracting gum disease significantly.[29]

And, yes, you could look at your phone while you brush your teeth.

But why would you?

Curate Curation

One of the things that distorts our exercise regimen and attitudes toward our own bodies is an obsessive curating of self-image. Editing images of the self online creates unrealizable expectations, especially for young adults. This leads us toward poor goal-setting and possible injury.

→　CURATION PRACTICE

Limit your self-curation both for your own sake and for the sake of the younger people in your life who are particularly susceptible. Try to go for a given period of time without editing photos of yourself or your loved ones. Examine how you feel after this self-curation diet.

Look Up

Chiropractors now recognize a phenomenon called *text neck* caused by looking down at your phone too much.[30]

Text neck can lead to an array of symptoms ranging from a chronic, nagging pain to sharp, severe upper-back muscle spasms.

If a cervical nerve becomes pinched, pain and possibly neurological symptoms can radiate down your arm and into your hand.

Knit
like Christo

Knitting improves fine motor skills, sharpens the mind, and can actually reduce the incidence of arthritis and digital tremors. After a little practice the average knitter can make a 4 foot [1.2 m] scarf in about 8 hours (though of course speed depends on needle and yarn size).[31] What could you do if after mastering the basics you made knitting your regular practice? Ten years of device-free time would give you 14,000 hours, enough time for you to wrap Liberty Island with your handiwork in the style of the artist Christo. In fact, you'd even have enough time left to knit Lady Liberty her own scarf.

But seriously—in a 2011 study, researchers at the Mayo Clinic interviewed a random sample of 1,321 people ages seventy to eighty-nine about the cognitive activities they engaged in late in life. The study, published in the *Journal of Neuropsychiatry & Clinical Neurosciences*, found that those who engaged in crafts like knitting and crocheting had a diminished chance of developing cognitive impairment and memory loss.[32]

Fix It, Don't Get It Fixed

Oftentimes we hire out the solving of our problems to others in order to create more time for ourselves.

But in the age of the smartphone, we end up using those reclaimed hours to stare at our devices.

In the process, we waste time and opportunity.

Fixing things ourselves improves manual dexterity, focuses attention, and saves money.

IV.
Strengthening Love, Friendships, and Family

We are primates—social animals who evolved and succeeded by developing civilizations based on complex relationships.

Relationships are feedback mechanisms—give-and-take systems where we constantly look for affirmation from our friends and family to understand who we are.

Being secure and happy in our lives is strongly linked to how we feel we're being heard and seen by others and how we in turn hear and see them.

If this is what we truly want then we must focus on developing empathy above all things. This should be the guiding principle in how we use technology and how we instruct younger people in using it.

And we have much work to do. Recent studies indicate that markers for empathy among college students have declined by 40 percent in the last 30 years, more or less in sync with the emergence of online communication.[33]

Some have suggested that an app might be developed to remind people to be more empathetic.

But as the psychologist Sherry Turkle wisely puts it, "We are the empathy app."[34]

Love

With the 1,400 hours a year you'd have after giving up your smartphone, you'd have sufficient time to have sex with your partner nearly 16,000 times (assuming you're like most humans and your lovemaking sessions last an average of 5.4 minutes).[35]

REALITY CHECK

A 2018 study of romantic relationships among college students in the journal *Psychology of Popular Media Culture* found that "smartphone dependency is significantly linked to relationship uncertainty" and that "partners' perceived smartphone dependency predicts less relationship satisfaction."[36] According to a 2016 study, around a third of those surveyed said they would rather give up sex for 3 months than give up their smartphone for a single week.[37] Still another study of 2,000 adults who live with their spouses found that the number one before-sleep activity was looking at phones.[38] Additionally, more than three quarters of survey respondents sleep with their phones within arm's reach, and more than a third of those surveyed said that their sex life had been negatively affected by having the phone in the bedroom.

Relate

But seriously, how would a phone-reduced life allow us to relate better to our partners? The couples therapist Katherine Stavrianopoulos believes that when spouses turn to devices, they do so as a way of "exiting the relationship"—that is, removing themselves from the emotional engagement that is the very basis of togetherness. She encourages couples to take a moment and ask themselves when they turn to their devices why they're doing so. Oftentimes it's because one member of the relationship feels they are being ignored, brushed aside, or that their problems are not being taken seriously. Being aware of that entryway into device use is the first step toward disabling the device's pernicious effect upon your intimacy.

$\longrightarrow$ RELATING PRACTICE

Have the last interaction before bedtime be a real-time exchange of words and looks with your partner—a short check-in where you are consciously trying to focus on each other's words and needs. This may not be possible to do every night, but try at least once a week. Reflect back on this "good-night acknowledgment" during other days of the week and try to keep that feeling of connectedness with you.

Feel the Complexity of "Imperfection"

Phones give us the illusion that touch should be perfection. A smooth surface with no resistance.

But this isn't perfection.

It's brute simplicity.

Next time you touch your partner or shake hands with a friend or pat your child on the head, take a moment to experience the complexity of touch, the lack of smoothness, the "imperfection."

There's much more to it than glass.

"I have this not-unserious theory that smartphones are going to extinct the human race because all the adolescents I know who have grown up with them are uncomfortable touching other human beings."
—Rowan Jacobsen, James Beard Award–winning author of *A Geography of Oysters*[39]

Redirect Distraction Toward Compassion

In recent years the tech community has come to embrace "mindfulness" meditation in part because the practice can increase focus and task-oriented concentration. But this limited approach risks stopping us short of the deeper work that meditation should engender.[40] As the Buddhist scholar Annabella Pitkin told me, "the insight into self is inextricable from compassion. If we really perceive how we and others truly exist, then compassion and loving-kindness naturally arise. We cultivate concentration, insight, and compassion in tandem, and they mutually reinforce."

The precise moment when distraction arises and leads you to your phone is a moment that you could reclaim for compassion. When the Buddhist meditation teacher and author Sylvia Boorstein is meeting a friend, she purposely doesn't take out her phone to pass the time while she waits. Instead, she looks at others around her and imagines thought bubbles over their heads with their particular suffering: Heartbreak. Anxiety. Despair. She wishes them release from their suffering. Follow Boorstein's example the next time you're passing time in a public place. Even if you eventually turn back to your phone, claiming at least one moment of compassionate thought for the suffering of others can begin to break the circular loop of distraction and self-involvement.

Call a Friend You're About to Text

Try to use texting just for logistical purposes, saving emotional information for more direct communication.

Or Better Yet, Meet in Person

Eye contact is the bedrock of empathy.

And When You Meet, Have an Unedited Conversation

Many people say they text or email rather than talk because they have come to fear the spontaneity of actual conversation.

They fear, above all, an awkward silence.

But "[i]t is often in the moments when we stumble and hesitate and fall silent that we reveal ourselves to each other," Sherry Turkle writes in *Reclaiming Conversation.*[41]

Choose to be revealed rather than false.

Even seemingly inert technology has the ability to disrupt. Sherry Turkle notes in her book *Alone Together* that studies consistently show "that if two people are having lunch a cell phone at the table steers the conversation to lighter subjects and each party feels less invested in the other."[42]

Don't Interrupt the Melody of Conversation with a Bad Tech Note

Observe the next time you find yourself in a good conversation with a friend or family member and note when that conversation is interrupted by a technological intrusion. A selfie. A show of photographs of other moments.

Remember that your conversation and the joy you are taking from it right now are precious and cannot be replicated at another moment in the future, regardless of whether or not you've preserved the moment in a photograph.

Next time you go to a live event, be it a rock concert or your child's school performance, instead of recording it, put down your phone and watch. Consciously remember details from the performance. Note those details back at dinner. A memory is worth a thousand pictures.

Value Real Friendships Over Virtual "Friends"

The social media use of the term *friend* is an appropriation that downplays the critical roles friends play in our lives. Most psychologists agree that humans can only effectively maintain a relatively small number of truly intimate friendships—usually around 15.[43] By this standard, having 1,000 "friends" is absurd. As you start to evaluate a less phone-centered life, take a long, hard look at your list of digital friends and cull the list to those with whom you have meaningful communication.

Say No to "Maybe"

When making plans, try to honor your commitments to your intimates. Make a plan and stick to it. Be respectful of the agreed-upon time you and your loved one have set aside to be together. Keeping commitments with your intimates is another bedrock of trustworthy relationships. The word "maybe" erodes trust and weakens the bonds of friendship. "Maybe" also ties you back to endless text chains while you wait for the "maybe" to become a "yes" or a "no." So next time you schedule something with a friend, make a plan, put down your phone, and say no to "maybe."

Practice Digital Right Speech

Whenever you text or post something, you are intruding upon another person's solitude, whether intentionally or unintentionally.

→ DIGITAL SPEECH PRACTICE

Before texting, posting, or making any other public statement, remember Gandhi's helpful saying: "Speak only if it improves upon silence."

Talk, in Person, to Those with Whom You Might Not Agree...

Because digital expression tends to be declarative rather than collaborative, curated rather than spontaneous, online political positions get stuck in a groove.

→   **TALK PRACTICE**

If you sense someone in your life holds opposing political views, invite that person to have an in-person conversation. While this might seem daunting, it's important to remember that in-person interaction is profoundly richer in information exchange than declarative, online posting. In one-on-one interactions, subtleties of information are conveyed through variations in vocal intonation, facial expression, and even smells and hormones that affect our emotional response. All of these forms of communication allow us to listen more deeply and react with greater empathy and subtlety.

Catch

The simple act of playing catch with a loved one engages both the mind and body and mandates eye contact. Eye contact, as it turns out, is the first and most essential brick in building a house of empathy. This is vital for the stability and well-being of both people in the relationship.

If two people played a game of catch that lasted the length of time you'd normally spend on your smartphone in a year, they would end up throwing a ball about 8,000 miles [12,874 km], or almost three times back and forth across the United States.

Look and Listen

Aside from a transcontinental game of catch, merely paying attention and having direct communication with eye contact is one of the best ways to teach empathy.

Empathy is a bilateral arrangement. Someone talks, someone listens. The knowledge of having been heard compels reciprocity and understanding.

As Adam Alter noted in his book *Irresistible*, "Empathy can't flourish without immediate feedback."[44]

Create a Culture within Your Family That Puts Technology in Its Proper Place

Instead of making technology something that gets given or taken away, do what author Jean Twenge suggests in her book *iGen* and create rituals for togetherness. Family dinners are obvious starting points for device-free time. Create a family digital policy with clear borders about when and where tech is allowed. Apply these borders equally to adults and children. I wish I had done this sooner in my family's history, but even now, 12 years in, I've seen that it can be done. Learn from my mistake. Establish rituals and borders as early in your child's life as possible so that it becomes part of your family's native culture.

Communicate Across Cultural Lines

One of the best ways to come to understand a different culture and the different way of thinking embedded within that culture is to develop proficiency in a new language.

According to the Common European Framework of Reference for Languages, it takes approximately 700 hours to reach the "C1 Advanced Level" in a foreign language.[45] Instead of staring into your smartphone without reply, you could spend your 1,400 hours learning two languages and begin communicating with a whole new range of people.

Communicate with Another Species Altogether

Three recent studies published in the *Journal of Personality and Social Psychology* found that pet owners have greater self-esteem, get more exercise, and are better at staving off negativity caused by social rejection.[46] The financial cost of dog ownership is about the same as owning a smart device. Cat ownership is even less. According to Adopt-a-Pet, North America's largest pet adoption website, the time cost is the same or less as smartphone ownership—3 to 4 hours a day for a dog and around 2 hours a day for a cat. And if you don't want the responsibility of ownership, just spending time with an animal by volunteering at a shelter or playing with a friend's pet can have positive health effects, including lower blood pressure and decreased levels of cortisol (a stress-related hormone).

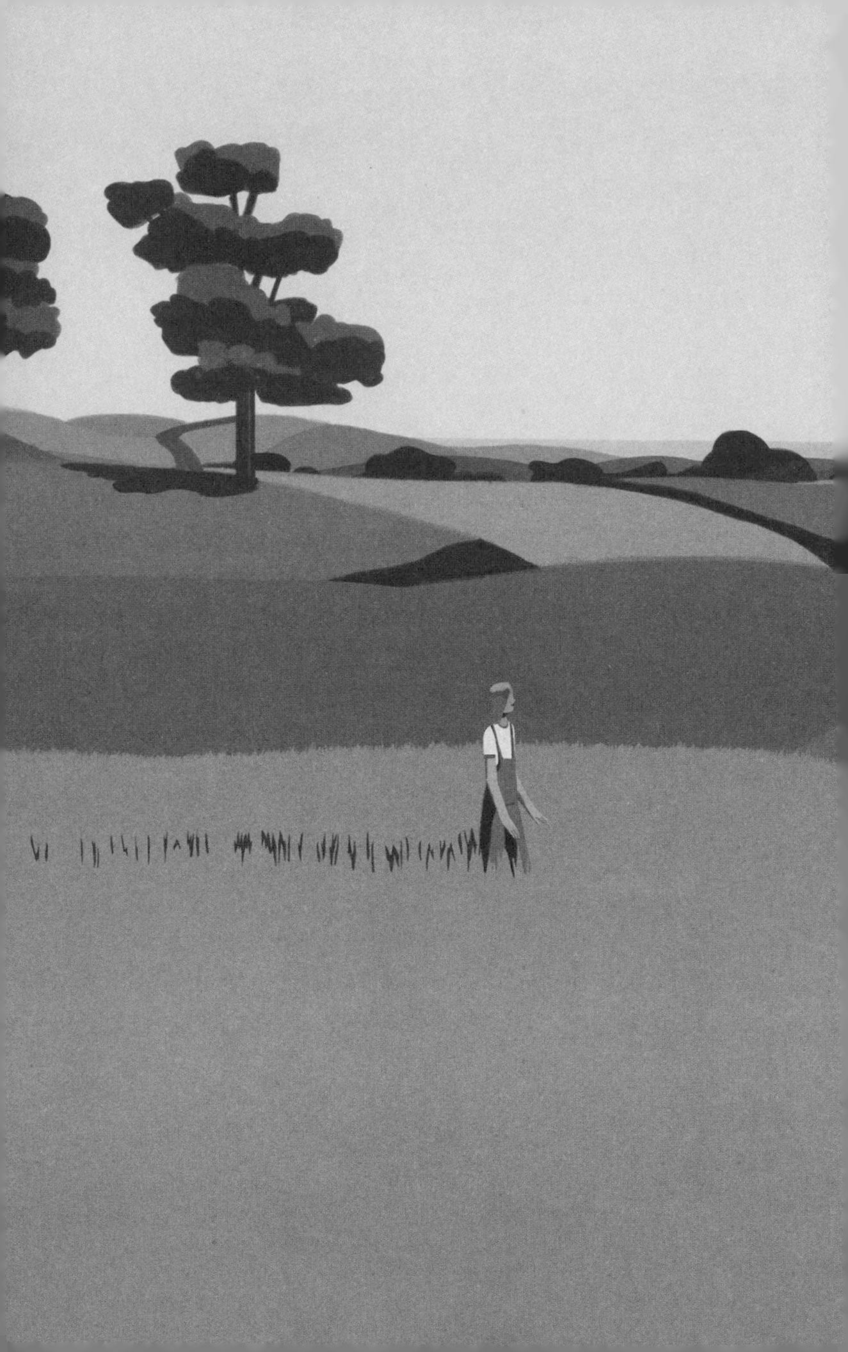

V.
Healing the Environment

There are many individual actions we can take to address the degradation of the natural world.

But before we can even consider those actions, we have to look with real eyes at the real world to see and feel how the globe's ecosystems are suffering.

It is through engagement with our physical environment that we take the first steps toward healing our planet.

See the World Slowly

The US National Forest system contains 98,400 miles [158,360 km] of nonmotorized trails available for hiking and encompasses around 193 million acres [78,104,328 ha] across forty-four states. Similar networks exist throughout the world.

If you repurposed your annual 1,400 hours of device time to hiking instead, you could cover 4,200 miles [6,759 km] in a year.[47] Over 20 years, that's close to the entirety of all trails in the entire US National Forest system. Across the Atlantic, that yearly amount of walking would take you nearly twice around the designated hiking mileage in the United Kingdom, and 13 months of device-free time would be enough for you to walk all 4,960 miles [7,982 km] of the E-1—the European Long Distance Path designated by the European Ramblers Association—a continuous footpath from northern Norway to Sicily.

Meanwhile, the money you'd save in a year of device quitting would be more than enough to fully equip you for a hiking or backpacking adventure, buy the necessary supplies, and pay for the transportation costs to get to and from the trailhead.

"Walk as if you are kissing the Earth with your feet."

—THICH NHAT HANH
IN *PEACE IS EVERY STEP*

Plant

Planting trees is by far the cheapest, most effective way to slow and possibly even reverse climate change. In 2019, the Crowther Lab at the Swiss Federal Institute of Technology in Zurich found that 2.2 billion acres [0.9 billion ha] are available on the planet for reforestation.[48] These new forests could store 205 billion tons [186 tonnes] of carbon or about two-thirds of the 300 billion tons [277 tonnes] humans have released into the atmosphere since the Industrial Revolution. The greatest potential can be found in just six countries: Russia (373 million acres [151 million ha]); the US (255 million acres [103 million ha]); Canada (194 million acres [78.4 million ha]); Australia (143 million acres [58 million ha]); Brazil (123 million acres [49.7 million ha]); and China (99 million acres [40.2 million ha]).

In those six countries, approximately ⅔ acre [¼ ha] of degraded land can often be purchased for less than the 10-year cost of owning a smartphone. In other words, if every smartphone owner in those countries put down their phone and bought and reforested a quarter hectare of land, we could make huge strides toward solving the climate crisis.

Clean

Plastic pollution is one of the greatest threats to the global oceans today. Every year, around 10 million tons of plastic waste flows into the seas of the world. According to George Leonard at the nonprofit Ocean Conservancy, if Americans applied their smartphone time to beach cleanup at the organization's recorded average rate of 5 pounds [2.3 kg] of plastic garbage per person per hour, "the volunteer effort could clean up the amount of plastic that lands on beaches 118 times over."[49]

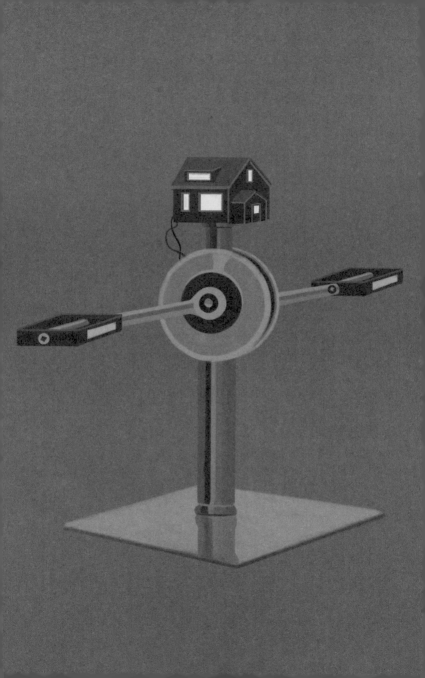

Generate

If each member of an average four-person household were to ride an electricity-generating exercise bike for an hour a day for a year instead of staring at a phone, they would produce 146 kilowatts of power, or 1.6 percent of that family's yearly energy needs.[50] If every smartphone-using family did this, we humans would burn 200 billion pounds [90 billion kg] less coal per year.

Bradley Whaley of Pedal Power Generators can equip you with an electricity generating bike for about $700. Pedal Power can also advise you on building a DIY generator bike for about $250, so you could potentially get four bikes and turn your whole family into a generator for less than the price of a year's worth of smartphone usage.

Stop Idling

Distracted behavior while on phones often leads to irresponsible behavior elsewhere in our lives. Take the example of sitting in your car, looking at your phone, and forgetting to turn off your car engine. According to the environmental law scholar Jason Czarnezki, engine idling accounts for 1.6 percent of all US carbon dioxide emissions and 10.6 billion gallons [more than 40 billion L] of fuel per year.[51] Addressing idling in the United States would prevent as much as 106 million tons [96 million tonnes] of carbon dioxide emissions going into the atmosphere. Perhaps this is why more progressive countries like France have imposed hefty fines on engine idlers that can exceed $545 [€500].

Shut Down Instead of Stand By

When our devices are in "sleep mode," they are so easily woken up again that we often dive right back in without questioning the need for yet another digital moment. To clear out space for offline thought, fully shut down devices and computers at the end of the day. There's also an environmental reason to fully shut down. Standby power, also called "vampire power," accounts for as much as 10 percent of residential energy use in developed countries,[52] spewing about 254 million tons [230 million tonnes] of carbon into the atmosphere every year.[53] By fully shutting down devices at the end of the day, you could drive a small stake into the vampire's heart. Shut down your internet router at day's end and you'll drive that stake even deeper.

Look at the Night Sky

A 2003 UC Irvine study found that people who experienced "vastness and awe" expanded their worldview and tended to "forego strict self-interest to improve the welfare of others."[54] Research subjects also felt they had more time available, were less impatient, and preferred experiences over material products.

→   NIGHT SKY PRACTICE

Thanks to the International Dark-Sky Association, you can find "dark reserves" in nine different countries.[55] Next time you plan a family vacation, why not choose one of these reserves for an overnight or two? Replace screen time with star time, and rediscover the vastness above.

Motivate

Currently, political leaders in the US and several other countries, including the UK and Canada, are elected from a vote organized by place, such as states or congressional districts, instead of by people. As a result, the candidate or party that the most people vote for often loses the election. As David Gold, the director of the nonprofit organization Democratism told me, this defect could be removed if citizens of these nations pressed their local representatives to force a change to their national election systems.[56] "Quitting devices for a year," Gold continued, "would give citizens enough time and money to visit their local representatives three times a week for a year and cover the cost of the trip in gas or mass transit to demand reform."

REALITY CHECK

According to the United States Public Interest Research Group (USPIRG), the best way to get leaders to change course is to visit them in person. "If they have town halls, go to them," USPIRG advises. "Go to their local offices. If you're in Washington, DC, try to find a way to go to their events. Go to the 'mobile offices' that their staff hold periodically (these times can often be found on each congressperson's website). When you go, ask questions—a lot of them. And push for answers. The louder, more vocal, and [more] present you can be at those events, the better."[57]

Get Lost

David de Rothschild didn't know how to sail a boat, but he built a ship out of plastic bottles, named it *Plastiki*, and sailed it across the Pacific as a way of bringing awareness to ocean plastic pollution. In the process, he learned about the value of getting lost. In a letter de Rothschild wrote me reflecting on the experience, he explained:

"We're the first generation who can never be lost. We're fearful of getting lost, but we are so lost. Asking the right questions and not being scared of the answers are fundamental to being a lost explorer. It is the path to true resilience and how to future-proof yourself. Getting lost is being open to possibility and magic. It's also being open to creating change."

Disappear

The other side of getting lost is disappearing altogether, at least in a digital sense.

→   DISAPPEARING PRACTICE

Take a few minutes each day to erase your stored internet cookies and search histories.

REALITY CHECK

A 2018 *New York Times* investigation showed how apps, without user knowledge, tracked users to Planned Parenthood clinics, Weight Watchers meetings, and intentionally discreet personal encounters. "Location information can reveal some of the most intimate details of a person's life—whether you've visited a psychiatrist, whether you went to an AA meeting, who you might date," said Senator Ron Wyden, Democrat of Oregon, who has proposed bills to limit the collection and sale of such data, which are largely unregulated in the United States. "It's not right to have consumers kept in the dark about how their data is sold and shared and then leave them unable to do anything about it."[58]

VI.
Healing Your Environment

None of the suggestions I've made so far will work unless you begin to take control of how technology infringes upon your time and your thoughts.

Remember, the technology industry has a vested interest in distracting you and keeping your attention on their products rather than your well-being.

You must develop and deploy a strategy to create your own island of deep thought and conscious action.

Don't Make Your Homescreen Your Home

We have all felt that desperate longing before we turn to our screens. That feeling that our homescreen is our true home. But your homescreen is not your home; it is a constructed environment influenced by marketers and programmers to feel like a safe place.

Curate your tech in a way that minimizes the comfort of that home and the intrusions on your consciousness that come with it.

Remember that any time a communication channel is open, it will be used by marketers to reach you. And because tech companies employ fleets of programmers to analyze what keeps you clicking, they will work extremely hard to keep you online once you engage.

Make your homescreen less
"homey" and curate your space
to minimize intrusion:

- Have a specific place in your home
  where laptops and phones charge.

- Introduce "speed bumps," as
  Catherine Price calls them in
  How to Break Up with Your Phone—
  methods of your own design that
  slow your path back onto devices.
  Stow apps inside folders so that
  more than one click is necessary
  to access them. Set up a vacation
  reply for your text messages to
  impede the compulsion to reply
  immediately. Remove your browser,
  messaging, and email programs
  from your laptop dock.[59]

- Remove as many bookmarks from your browser as possible.

- Build pauses at every turn to prevent unconscious transition from directed tasks to undirected wandering.

- Keep a handwritten list of things you want to look up in a future internet session and do your searching with intentionality.

Don't Let a Device Navigate a Landscape You Already Know

The stickiest, most difficult-to-avoid things on our phones are map applications. But they don't have to be. While sometimes necessary in unfamiliar territory, map apps undermine our knowledge of the things we actually know by heart. There is no need to use a map app in your own town, and especially not in your own neighborhood.

Crossing into familiar territory should be a cue to turn off your phone.

*"Landscape recalls you into
a mindful mode of stillness,
solitude, and silence where you
can truly receive time."*

—JOHN O'DONOHUE, CELTIC POET,
FORMER PRIEST,
HEGELIAN PHILOSOPHER[60]

Create an Archipelago of Unconnected Places

The default for most modern locations is cell phone reception, Wi-Fi access, and often a public screen displaying a mix of content and advertising. Understand that you cannot avoid this entirely but can seek out places in the different parts of your day that buck the trend. They exist. Make visiting these places part of your daily routine. Look for one of the increasing number of coffee shops that don't have Wi-Fi access. If you live in a waterfront city, consider commuting by ferry—many ferries still float free of the internet. Parks, though sometimes wired, still contain many free zones.

Don't Let Your Mind Eat Junk

Many critics of the tech industry draw an analogy between device overuse and the consumption of junk food.

In the 1950s, when highly processed food first appeared, humans didn't know how bad much of that food could be for our bodies. So the default was to eat it.

Same thing with the vast majority of what's available on your device: junk. But we eat it.

If we'd instead defaulted to not eating processed foods, wouldn't our bodies be a lot healthier? If we make the default not to consume junk media, wouldn't our minds be in better shape, too?

Make Your Tech Stupider So You Can Be Smarter

Tech can of course augment our abilities in some ways, helping us accomplish tasks more quickly or efficiently. But there are many cases where tech poses solutions to problems that we can easily accomplish on our own. And when we default to digital solutions to problems our brains can solve, we atrophy critical parts of our minds.

We need to make wise choices and dumb down our tech to give the brain a chance to assert its true power.

A few thoughts on how to do this:

Make your smartphone stupid. Disable your web browser. Instructions can be easily found, on, well, the internet. While you're at it, delete your mail app, too. Most messages can wait. Rushed, unthoughtful responses just generate more messages of apology or correction later on.

Or abandon the smartphone altogether and use a flip phone. I did, and after a year, I have yet to suffer any loss of income or connectedness with my friends and family.

If you can't stomach abandoning your smartphone, Cal Newport in his book *Digital Minimalism* suggests trying out the Light Phone—a pared down device that links to your smartphone, allowing you to leave home without digital baggage.[61]

Or next time you upgrade to a new computer, downgrade your old computer to an unconnected device for quieter work.

Try doing some analog research and see where it leads. That's what the bestselling author Laura Hillenbrand does. Hillenbrand suffers from a kind of vertigo that requires her to do all of her research on paper.[62] While going through old newspapers when she was researching her bestseller *Seabiscuit,* she happened upon the story of one Louie Zamperini, who, after being an Olympic champion in the 1932 Berlin games, harrowingly survived being shot down over the Pacific, weeks at sea in a raft, and years in a Japanese POW camp. That story ended up being the basis of her next, even more bestselling book *Unbroken.*

Curate Your Life, Not Your Image

In 1954, the authors Scott and Helen Nearing wrote *Living the Good Life*, a book that is often called the spark that started the back-to-the-land movement.[63] Over the course of their long lives, they hand-built two houses, learned to subsistence farm, and produced books and articles that influenced millions of people.

The key to this couple's meditative productivity was dividing their days into three parts:

1. BREAD LABOR

The time they spent on work to sustain themselves economically. If you are a homemaker, work to maintain your household should be included in this time.

2. VOCATIONAL ACTION

A practice like I outlined at the beginning of this book—music, poetry, painting—or an activity that feeds the deepest creative aspirations of the soul.

3. COMMUNITY BUILDING

Work aimed at the betterment of society overall.

Though the Nearings' purity of purpose is a high bar to reproduce, it is a useful framework for organizing your day away from non-focused device time. Planning your day along these cardinal points leads you to question unproductive time and can motivate you to gravitate toward right action.

Check for Tics

In cognitive behavioral therapy, psychologists train patients to take note of behaviors or thoughts that send them off on compulsive, non-reality-based trains of thought. By identifying the harbingers of distracted behavior and noting when they arise, patients can gradually halt spirals of negative thought and lead more productive lives.

The same can hold true for overactive device use.

Maybe it's a piece of music you hear that makes you want to look up the songwriter.

Maybe it's a worrying need to see how a post did on Twitter.

Whatever it is, note it next time you reach for your device. Note the physical cues and your emotional state that compelled you to reach into your pocket. Identify those cues; name them. Remember these labels and cues next time you reach to check. Practiced over time, you can come to understand what is necessary and what is obsessive.

Question "Busyness"

Since the smartphone appeared, the notion that we are all extremely busy has become a common trope in conversation. "I'm crazy busy," a friend will say, or "So busy, can I get back to you later?" or "Super busy now, let's talk next week." But the statistics on smartphone use show that we are not that busy. We are just on our phones. Of the roughly 4 hours we spend on our phones each day, about three quarters of that is on social media and other nonessential, distracted activities.

Given that on-screen reading requires us to subconsciously make hundreds of tiny decisions per hour (see page 49), it's reasonable to suspect that what we are experiencing is not actual busyness and shortness of time but rather the *impression* of busyness. It's worth reflecting on this next time you think about where you could possibly find more time to do the things you love or spend time with the people you care about.

Demystify Novelty

Understand that novelty itself is addictive. Apps and notifications deliver random rewards that keep us forever searching for something new. Technology companies have designed their products around this essential premise.

But examine your heart and imagine the possibilities that newness might bring, and you will see that nothing truly satisfying is likely to be waiting behind that next click.

REALITY CHECK

"Slot machines make more money in the United States than baseball, movies, and theme parks combined. Relative to other kinds of gambling, people get 'problematically involved' with slot machines 3–4x faster . . . But here's the unfortunate truth—several billion people have a slot machine in their pocket: When we pull our phone out of our pocket, we're *playing a slot machine* to see what notifications we got. When we pull to refresh our email, we're *playing a slot machine* to see what new email we got."
—Tristan Harris, ex-Google design ethicist[64]

Keep What's Private Truly Private

How many times have friends told you something significant that happened in their lives—something that seemed deeply personal? How many times have you later found out that your friends have posted those same significant details of their lives online?

How does that make you feel?

Private thoughts, feelings, and moments are the currency of relationships.

Give them their proper value by sharing them exclusively with the people who share your trust and love.

Claim Your "Right to Disconnect"

In 2017, the French government passed Article 55(1), amending its labor code with *le droit à la déconnexion* or the "Right to Disconnect."[65] The law requires that companies with more than fifty employees designate hours when staff should not send or answer emails. Until you are protected by such laws at your own workplace, try to bring these issues up with your coworkers. And bosses, take note: Many studies show that allowing workers to disconnect and recharge tends to lead to greater productivity. The smartphone is a gateway to endless work. Workers should have the right to close the gate.

Everybody's Not Doing It

Just as the idea of eliminating bullying in schools or ending smoking in public spaces once seemed unrealizable, reining in technology's domineering presence in our minds also seems difficult to achieve.

But look around—more and more people are putting down their phones and taking back their lives.

As Shoshana Zuboff writes in her book *The Age of Surveillance Capitalism*, "It is not ok to have our best instincts for connection, empathy, and information exploited by a draconian quid pro quo that holds these goods hostage to the pervasive strip search of our lives. It is not ok for every move, emotion, utterance, and desire to be catalogued, manipulated, and then used to surreptitiously herd us through the future tense for the sake of someone else's profit."[66]

We need to talk to each other about this, and we need to talk about it in person, face-to-face. The writer Jia Tolentino quite rightly points out that "to speak out against something within the confines of the attention economy is, inevitably, to bring it more attention."[67]

So don't bring the attention economy any more attention. Put down your tech, and talk about your problems one-on-one with friends and family. It's the most human thing you can do.

"[Humans], it has been well said, think in herds. It will be seen that they go mad in herds, while they only recover their senses slowly, and one by one."

—CHARLES MACKAY IN
*EXTRAORDINARY POPULAR DELUSIONS
AND THE MADNESS OF CROWDS*

Afterword

"Krishna, my delusion is destroyed.
And by your grace
I have regained memory."

—ARJUNA TO KRISHNA,
THE BHAGAVAD GITA

I lie in bed with my twelve-year-old,
reading to him and talking about the day.

I wonder how many more evenings I'll
be asked to join this nighttime ritual.

I know the days of chats like this are numbered.

He has growing up to do.

But as I read to him or talk with him or laugh
with him, I realize that I, too, am experiencing
a transitional moment, along with every adult
at this time in history—a crisis in maturity.
We must weigh the evidence and choose
wisely for the sake of our future.

We are being swept down rapids of shifting
consciousness while desperately trying to
hold on to the rock of what is human.

Trying to be compassionate and
empathetic in the face of device
culture that makes us cold and cutoff.

The futurists, post-humanists, artificial
intelligence–boosters, and philosophers
of all stripes will call me a Luddite, I'm sure.

They assure us that some other
form of humanity waits for us
around technology's corner.

Something different.
Something bigger than human.

I am fairly sure that whatever this next
thing is, it will not be human in the way
I and most humans define humanity.

Some say we don't have much time left to be us.

Some say our species' dharma has run its course.

That may be true.

But I refuse to fold to that inevitability.

All I have are my basic human qualities:
my ability to love, empathize, experience, and
explore. These are things I choose to do with
my own two eyes, looking up at the night sky.

I lie here with my son, eighth grade just
around the corner.

He's just read what you've just read.

I ask him, after reading all this, if he really
wants to give his thoughts over to people and
corporations that don't care a bit about his
welfare.

I try to use what little bit of influence I still
have over him.

But ultimately the choice is his.

It is, after all, his time.

Endnotes

1. Sarah Myruski et al., "Digital disruption? Maternal mobile device use is related to infant social-emotional functioning." *Developmental Science* 21, no. 4 (September 2017).

2. Yoram Wurmser, "US Time Spent with Mobile 2019," *eMarketer* (May 2019).

3. Olivia Solon, "Ex-Facebook president Sean Parker: site made to exploit human 'vulnerability,'" *Guardian* (November 9, 2017), www.theguardian.com/technology/2017/nov/09/facebook-sean-parker-vulnerability-brain-psychology.

4. V. Rideout, M. B. Robb, "The Common Sense Census: Media Use by Tweens and Teens, 2019," Common Sense Media (2019), and Pew Research Center, "Spring 2018 Global Attitudes Survey," Q45 and Q46.

5. Rideout and Robb, "The Common Sense Census: Media Use by Tweens and Teens, 2019."

6. The Egyptian pharaoh Hatshepsut derived most of her wealth from gold mines that *Money* magazine valued at $2 billion in today's dollars. Kerry Close, "The 10 Richest Women of All Time," *Money* (February 1, 2016), https://money.com/10-richest-women-all-time/. By way of comparison, as of December 2019, the Bloomberg Billionaires Index estimated Mark Zuckerberg's wealth at $75.2 billion. www.bloomberg.com/billionaires/.

7. Gladwell's original description of the 10,000 hour rule (drawn originally from the Ericsson/Charness study; endnote 9) appears in his book *Outliers* (Boston: Little Brown and Company, 2008). After much criticism, Gladwell made this clarification of the 10,000 hour rule in a 2014 "Ask Me Anything" session on Reddit, https://www.reddit.com/r/IAmA/comments/2740ct/hi_im_malcolm_gladwell_author_of_the_tipping/.

8. Gloria Mark, Daniela Gudith, Ulrich Klocke, "The Cost of Interrupted Work: More Speed and Stress," Proceedings of the 2008 Conference on Human Factors in Computing Systems, CHI 2008, 2008, Florence, Italy, April 5–10, 2008.

9. The original citation for this much-cited article is K. Anders Ericsson, Neil K. Charness, "Expert Performance: Its Structure and Acquisition," *American Psychologist* 49, no. 7 (August 1994): 725–47.

10. Summarized from Stephen Cope, *The Great Work of Your Life: A Guide for the Journey to Your True Calling* (New York: Bantam Books, 2015), 162.

11. Harvard Medical School, "Blue Light has a Dark Side." *Harvard Health Letter*, first published May 2012, updated August 2018.

12. From Carl Jung, *Psychology and Alchemy* (Princeton: Princeton University Press, 1980), 45.

13. Cal Newport, *Digital Minimalism: Choosing a Focused Life in a Noisy World* (New York: Penguin, 2019), 133.

14. The so-called "paper clip test" is described in Joy Paul Guilford, *The Nature of Human Intelligence* (New York: McGraw-Hill, 1967).

15. From act 1, scene 1 of *King Lear* by William Shakespeare.

16. The most recent large meta-analysis of adult reading speed put the average at 238 words per minute, but many authors note that significant portions of the population read as slowly as 100 words per minute. As an imperfect compromise I've rounded down to 200. See Marc Brysbaert, "How many words do we read per minute? A review and meta-analysis of reading rate," *Journal of Memory and Language* 109 (December 2019).

17. Avni Bavishi, Martin D. Slade, Becca R. Levy, "A chapter a day: Association of book reading with longevity," *Social Science and Medicine* 164 (2016): 44–48.

18. Pablo Delgados, Cristina Vargas, Rakefet Ackerman; Ladislao Salmerón, "Don't throw away your printed books: A meta-analysis on the effects of reading media on reading comprehension," *Educational Research Review* 25 (November 2018): 23–38.

19. Catherine Price, *How to Break Up with Your Phone* (New York: Ten Speed Press, 2018), 57.

20. Vladimir Nabokov, *Lectures on Literature* (New York: Harcourt, 1980), 3.

21. Martin Dresler et al., "Mnemonic Training Reshapes Brain Networks to Support Superior Memory." *Neuron* 93 (March 2017): 1227–35.

22. Britta K. Hölzel et al., "Mindfulness practice leads to increases in regional brain gray matter density," *Psychiatry Research: Neuroimaging* 191, no. 1 (January 2011): 36–43.

23. While it is difficult to compare an organic processor (the brain) to the power of a computer, A. Sandberg and N. Bostrum suggested a range of 1018 (one exaFLOP) to 1025 FLOPS. See A. Sandberg, N.A. Bostrom, "Whole Brain Emulation: A Roadmap, Technical Report." #2008-3, Future of Humanity Institute, Oxford University.

24. Mayo Clinic, "Exercise: A drug-free approach to lowering high blood pressure," 2019, www.mayoclinic.org/diseases-conditions/high-blood-pressure/in-depth/high-blood-pressure/art-20045206.

25. As cited in Michael Gregor, *How Not to Die* (New York: Flatiron Books, 2015), 5.

26. The author of this yet-to-be published study discusses his findings here: https://theconversation.com/would-we-be-better-off-if-we-sent-email-into-retirement-34101.

27. For the details of Beaumont's around-the-world-in-less-than-80-days feat see BBC News, "Cyclist Mark Beaumont breaks around the world record," September 18, 2017, https://www.bbc.com/news/uk-scotland-tayside-central-41308524.

28. Arnold Schwarzenegger and Douglas Kent Hall, Arnold: *The Education of a Bodybuilder* (New York: Simon and Schuster, 1993), 179.

29. Andrew Gallagher et al., "The Effect of Brushing Time and Dentifrice on Dental Plaque Removal in Vivo." *Journal of Dental Hygiene 83*, no. 3 (June 2009): 111–16.

30. Jason M. Cuéllar, Todd H. Landman, "Text Neck: An Epidemic of the Modern Era of Cell Phones?" *Spine Journal 17*, no. 6 (June 2017): 901-2.

31. To my knowledge there has not been a scientific study of scarf knitting speed so I have drawn my numbers from a knitting forum on the site Craftster.org: https://www.craftster.org/forum/index.php?topic=70250.0.

32. Y. E. Geda et al, "Engaging in cognitive activities, aging, and mild cognitive impairment: a population-based study," *Journal of Neuropsychiatry and Clinical Neuroscience* 23, no. 2 (Spring 2012): 149–54.

33. Sarah H. Konrath, Edward H. O'Brien, Courtney Hsing, "Changes in Dispositional Empathy in American College Students Over Time: A Meta-Analysis," *Personality and Social Psychology Review* (August 2010): 180–98.

34. From Sherry Turkle, *Reclaiming Conversation: The Power of Talk in a Digital Age* (New York: Penguin Press, 2015), 126.

35. M. D. Waldinger et al. "A Multinational Population Survey of Intra-vaginal Ejaculation Latency Time," *Journal of Sexual Medicine* 2, no. 4 (July 2005): 492–97.

36. Matthew A. Lapierre, Meleah N. Lewis, "Should it stay or should it go now? Smartphones and relational health," *Psychology of Popular Media Culture* 7, no. 3 (2018): 384–98.

37. Delvv Digital Habits 2016 Survey Findings, www.delvv.com/downloads/survey_2016_results.pdf.

38. Based on a survey of 2,000 adults carried out in 2018 by OnePoll. Asurion, "The Goodnight Kiss Is Dead" (July 25, 2018), https://www.asurion.com/about/press-releases/the-goodnight-kiss-is-dead/.

39. From a personal email to the author.

40. The Stanford neurologist James Doty writes frequently about the hazards of failing to incorporate compassion into mindfulness training. See James R. Doty, *Into the Magic Shop: A Neurosurgeon's Quest to Discover the Mysteries of the Brain and the Secrets of the Heart* (New York: Avery, 2017).

41. Sherry Turkle, *Reclaiming Conversation: The Power of Talk in a Digital Age* (New York: Penguin Press, 2015), 323.

42. Sherry Turkle, *Alone Together: Why We Expect More From Technology and Less From Each Other* (New York: Basic Books, 2017), xxi.

43. W. X. Zhou, D. Sornett, R. A. Hill, R. I. M. Dunbar, "Discrete hierarchical organization of social group sizes," *Proceedings of the Royal Society B: Biological Sciences 272*, no. 1561 (February 2005).

44. Adam Alter, *Irresistible: The Rise of Addictive Technology and the Business of Keeping Us Hooked* (New York: Penguin Press, 2017), 40.

45. Cambridge Assessment English, "How many hours do I need to prepare for my exam," https://support.cambridgeenglish.org/hc/en-gb/articles/202838506-Guided-learning-hours.

46. Allen R. McConnell et al., "Friends with Benefits: On the Positive Consequences of Pet Ownership," *Journal of Personality and Social Psychology* 101, no. 6 (2011): 1239–52.

47. This is distilled from a December 2018 email exchange with Wes Swaffar, Director of Reforestation Programs and Partnerships, The National Forest Foundation.

48. Details of where and how much land could be reforested can be found in Jean-Francois Bastin et al., "The Global Tree Restoration Potential," *Science* 365, no. 6448 (July 2019): 76–79.

49. These numbers are distilled from a December 2018 email exchange with George Leonard of the nonprofit Ocean Conservancy. More information for ocean cleanup volunteer programs can be found at https://oceanconservancy.org/trash-free-seas/international-coastal-cleanup/.

50. Statistics on electricity-generating human drive trains come from a telephone interview with Bradley Whaley of Pedal Power. Those interested can order instructions or products from Pedal Power at www.pedalpowergenerator.com.

51. Jason Czarnezki, *Everyday Environmentalism: Law, Nature and Individual Behavior* (Washington, DC: Environmental Law Institute Press, 2011).

52. The US Department of Energy estimated a range of 5 to 10 percent in 2009. More details here: https://www.energy.gov/energysaver/articles/please-stand-reduce-your-standby-power-use.

53. 423.4 kilowatt hours per person per year from phantom power x 1.2 billion people in industrialized countries x 1 pound of carbon per kilowatt hour = 525,600,000,000 pounds, or 238,909,090 metric tons.

54. D. Keltner, J. Haidt, "Approaching awe, a moral, spiritual, and aesthetic emotion." *Cognitive Emotions* 17, no. 2 (March 2003): 297–314.

55. Those interested in locating a dark-sky preserve can search at https://www.darksky.org/our-work/conservation/idsp/reserves/.

56. More information about David Gold's work to reform voting and representation can found at www.democratism.org.

57. Read more at https://uspirg.org/resources/usp/call-your-representative-and-senators-every-day-heres-how.

58. Jennifer Valentino-DeVries, Natasha Singer, Michael H. Keller, Aaron Krolik, "Your Apps Know Where You Were Last Night, and They're Not Keeping It Secret," *New York Times* (December 10, 2018).

59. Catherine Price makes frequent mention of the useful term "speed bumps" as a way of defusing the digressive traps mobile media sets for us in *How to Break Up with Your Phone* (Berkeley, CA: Ten Speed Press, 2018).

60. Radio interview by Krista Tippett with John O'Donohue, *On Being* (August 31, 2017). https://onbeing.org/programs/john-odonohue-the-inner-landscape-of-beauty-aug2017/.

61. More information on the Light Phone can be found at www.thelight-phone.com/products.

62. Wil S. Hylton, "The Unbreakable Laura Hillenbrand," *New York Times Magazine* (December 18, 2014).

63. Helen and Scott Nearing first gave account of their directed, three-part day in *Living the Good Life: How to Live Sanely and Simply in a Troubled World*, originally self-published in 1954. They followed up with a sequel called *Continuing the Good Life* when they moved their subsistence farm from Vermont to Maine in the 1970s. Both books are now combined into a single volume: *The Good Life* (New York: Schocken Books, 1990).

64. Tristan Harris, "The Slot Machine in Your Pocket," *Der Spiegel* (July 27, 2016).

65. The statute (in French) can be found at https://www.legifrance.gouv.fr/affichCodeArticle.do?cidTexte=LEGITEXT000006072050&idArticle=LEGIARTI000033024095&dateTexte=&categorieLien=id.

66. Shoshana Zuboff, *The Age of Surveillance Capitalism: The Fight for a Human Future at the New Frontier of Power* (New York: PublicAffairs, 2019), 521.

67. Jia Tolentino, "What It Takes to Put Your Phone Away," *New Yorker* (April 22, 2019).

Select Bibliography

Aboulker-Muscat, Colette. *Encyclopedia of Mental Imagery*. New York: ACMI Press, 2012.

Alter, Adam. *Irresistible: The Rise of Addictive Technology and the Business of Keeping Us Hooked*. New York: Penguin Press, 2017.

Chödrön, Pema. *Start Where You Are: A Guide to Compassionate Living*. Boston: Shambhala, 2001.

———. *Taking the Leap: Freeing Ourselves from Old Habits and Fears*. Boston: Shambhala Publications, 2009.

———. *When Things Fall Apart: Heart Advice for Difficult Times*. Boston: Shambhala, 2000.

Cope, Stephen. *The Great Work of Your life: A Guide for the Journey to Your True Calling*. New York: Bantam Books, 2015.

Czarnezki, Jason. *Everyday Environmentalism*. Washington: Environmental Law Institute, 2013.

Furlong, Monica. *Zen Effects: The Life of Alan Watts*. Woodstock: Skylight Paths Publishing, 2001.

Goddard, Dwight, editor. *A Buddhist Bible*. Boston: Beacon Press, 1994.

Goldstein, Joseph. *Insight Meditation: The Practice of Freedom*. Boston: Shambhala, 2003.

Greger, Michael. *How Not to Die*. London: Pan Books, 2015.

Hanh, Thich Nhat. *Peace Is Every Step*. New York: Bantam Books, 1992.

Jung, Carl. *Psychology and Alchemy*. Princeton: Princeton University Press, 1980.

Miller, Barbara Stoler, translator. *The Bhagavad-Gita: Krishna's Counsel in the Time of War*. New York: Bantam Dell, 2004.

Mishra, Pankaj. *An End to Suffering: The Buddha in the World*. New York: Farrar, Straus, Giroux, 2004.

Mitchell, Stephen T, translator. *Tao Te Ching*. New York: Harper Perennial, 1988.

Nabokov, Vladimir. *Lectures on Literature*. New York: Harcourt, 1980.

Newport, Cal. *Digital Minimalism: Choosing a Focused Life in a Noisy World*. New York: Penguin, 2019.

Pollan, Michael. *How to Change Your Mind: What the New Science of Psychedelics Teaches Us About Consciousness, Dying, Addiction, Depression, and Transcendence*. New York: Penguin, 2018.

Powers, Richard. *The Overstory*. New York: W. W. Norton & Company, 2019.

Price, Catherine. *How to Break Up with Your Phone*. New York: Ten Speed Press, 2018.

Safina, Carl. *The View from Lazy Point: A Natural Year in an Unnatural World*. New York: Picador, 2012.

Schwarzenegger, Arnold and Hall, Douglas Kent. *Arnold: The Education of a Bodybuilder*. New York: Simon and Schuster, 1993.

Thoreau, Henry David. *Walden and Other Writings*. New York: The Modern Library, 2000.

Trevelyan, George Macaulay. *The Recreations of an Historian*. London: Thomas Nelson and Sons, 1919.

Turkle, Sherry. *Alone Together: Why We Expect More from Technology and Less from Each Other*. New York: Basic Books, 2017.

———. *Reclaiming Conversation: The Power of Talk in a Digital Age*. New York: Penguin Press, 2015.

Twenge, Jean. *iGen: Why Today's Super-Connected Kids Are Growing Up Less Rebellious, More Tolerant, Less Happy—and Completely Unprepared for Adulthood—and What That Means for the Rest of Us*. New York: Atria Books, 2017.

Zuboff, Shoshana. *The Age of Surveillance Capitalism: The Fight for a Human Future at the New Frontier of Power*. New York: PublicAffairs, 2019.

Acknowledgments

When writing acknowledgments for a book aimed at restoring calm and consciousness, one is tempted to thank the author of every contemplative text that has come one's way over the course of an entire life. But in the name of efficiency, I'll cull the list and share the names of the people and books that were most helpful in this particular journey. In the now extensive literature on device resistance, Cal Newport's *Digital Minimalism* stands out as a key text. Wise, practical, and engaging, it is a line in the sand that all parties in the tech fights ahead should heed. Likewise Sherry Turkle's works *Alone Together* and *Reclaiming Conversation* stand as vital living memories of our minds before the Great Erosion that tech has brought to our emotional lives. In the spheres of meditation and lovingkindness practice, a great thanks to Sylvia Boorstein for generously sharing both her personal and professional experiences. The writings of Stephen Cope and Pema Chödrön were similarly inspiring and motivating. Thanks also to the Sanskrit scholar and founder of the nonprofit Democratism, David Gold, for his help with interpretation of both *The Bhagavad Gita* and contemporary constitutional democracy. Also much gratitude to the author and illustrator Elisha Cooper for his sage advice as the book took shape and to the writer Peter Hirsch for his thoughts on wrapping islands with scarves and other whimsies. And to the Buddhist scholar Annabella Pitkin for her input on meditation, compassion, and sacred texts. Thanks as well are owed to Leah and Hannah Alpert, Russell Cohen, and David Jacobs for vetting the book over the course of many phases. Lastly, thanks to those early believers in this project when it was only an idea in the wind—Clay Risen, my sometimes editor at the *New York Times* Opinion Page, Carl Safina and The Safina Center, Meg Thompson and Cindy Uh at the Thompson Literary Agency, Rachel Hiles at Chronicle Books, and my life partner, Esther Drill. If Esther had a Homeric epithet attached to her name, it would be "Reader of Many Drafts."